Motion & Movement

Published by Creative Education
P.O. Box 227
Mankato, Minnesota 56002
Creative Education is an imprint of The Creative Company.

DESIGN AND PRODUCTION BY **ZENO DESIGN**

PHOTOGRAPHS BY Alamy (JUPITERIMAGES/STOCK IMAGE),
Gary Benson, Richard Cummins, David Davis, Getty Images
(Martin Harvey, Marcus Lyon, Kauro Mikami, Donald Miralle/
Staff, Patrick Trefz), The Image Finders (Jim Baron, Mark
E. Givson, Dave Haas, Greg Hildebrandt, Michael Philip
Manheim), Tom Myers Photography (Tom Myers, M. Nevins),
NASA, Tom Stack & Associates (Erwin & Peggy Bauer, Mike
Severns), Unicorn (Arni Katz, Mike Lepsch, Tom McCarthy,
Daniel J. Olson, Herbert L. Stormont)

LIBRARY OF CONGRESS CATALOGING-IN-PUBLICATION DATA

Frisch-Schmoll, Joy.
Motion and movement / by Joy Frisch-Schmoll.
p. cm. — (Simple science)
Includes index.
ISBN 978-1-58341-578-8
1. Motion—Juvenile literature. I. Title. II. Title: Motion and
movement. III. Series.

QC133.5.F75 2008
531'.11—dc22   2007004186

First edition

9 8 7 6 5 4 3 2

Motion & Movement

Joy Frisch–Schmoll

CREATIVE 🍎 EDUCATION

The world around us is always moving. Birds fly. Trucks move. People walk. We call this movement "motion." Motion happens when something changes place. A **force** is something that makes a thing move.

Cheetahs are the fastest land animals in the world. They have slim bodies. They need to be fast to catch other animals to eat.

LOTS OF FISH MOVE IN THE OCEAN

Nothing would ever happen without forces. Something has to push or pull an object to make it move. Leaves will blow off trees when the wind is strong. A book will not move by itself. Someone must pick it up.

THE WIND PUSHES ON TREE LEAVES

MOTION & MOVEMENT

Isaac Newton was a **scientist** (*SI-en-tist*) who lived a long time ago. He learned about motion. He learned why things move. Newton learned about **gravity** (*GRAV-eh-tee*), too.

There are more than 600 muscles in your body. The muscles pull on bones to make your body move.

GRAVITY PULLS THINGS DOWN

MOTION & MOVEMENT

People and animals have muscles that help them move. People use lots of muscles when they run and jump. Birds use their wings to push air down so they can fly up. Fish and other sea animals use tails and fins to move through water.

BIRDS FLAP THEIR WINGS TO GO UP

MOTION & MOVEMENT

When kids jump on a **trampoline** (*tram-puh-LEEN*), they push down. The trampoline pushes them back up. Swimmers kick water backward. This makes them move forward.

SWIMMERS KICK TO GO FORWARD

MOTION & MOVEMENT

Things that are heavy are hard to move.

A piano is heavy. Special machines or

tools make it easier to move heavy things.

A cart with wheels can be used to pull

heavy things. Wheels make it easier to

move things.

WHEELS HELP BIG MACHINES MOVE

MOTION & MOVEMENT

Friction (*FRIK-shen*) slows things down or stops them from moving. Friction is what happens when two things rub together. Sometimes friction is helpful. Friction slows down a bike when you use the brakes.

People can use friction to make fire. They can rub two sticks together. This makes the sticks get hot and start on fire.

BIKE BRAKES WORK USING FRICTION

MOTION & MOVEMENT

Sometimes friction is not helpful. It slows down things that need to go fast. Airplanes need to go fast. They have smooth surfaces to go through the air easily. Air makes friction by rubbing against things.

AIRPLANES ARE SMOOTH AND POINTY

Motion happens around us every day. Birds and animals move around. Kids throw balls. Things change place all the time. Motion makes the world a fun place!

Skis are smooth on the bottom. This lets skiers slide over snow easily. There would be a lot of friction if the skis were rough.

SOME KINDS OF MOTION ARE FUN

MOTION & MOVEMENT

To see how friction works, get a heavy book and a toy car. Put them on a smooth floor. Try to slide each one across the floor. The toy car will roll a long way. Only the wheels touch the floor. Friction stops the book from sliding far. A lot of the book touches the floor. Now slide the book and car on a floor with carpet. They will not go as far. There is more friction on carpet.

force a push or pull that makes something move

friction when two things rub together

gravity the force that pulls things down to Earth

scientist a person who learns about science

trampoline a stretchy sheet used for jumping and bouncing

23

24

airplanes **18**

bikes **16**

birds **4, 10, 20**

cheetahs **4**

fire **16**

forces **4, 6, 23**

friction **16, 18, 20, 22, 23**

gravity **8, 23**

muscles **8, 10**

Newton, Isaac **8**

swimmers **12**

trampolines **12, 23**

wheels **14, 22**